My Silly Book of
COLORS

Written by Susan Amerikaner
Illustrated by Judy Ziegler

SILVER PRESS

Amerikaner, Susan.
    My silly book of colors / by Susan Amerikaner;
illustrated by Judy Ziegler.
            p.   cm.
    Summary: Rhymed text and illustrations in-
troduce different colors through the antics of
various animals.
    [1. Colors.] I. Ziegler, Judy, III.   II. Title.
PZ7.4997My   1989
[E]—dc19   89-5976
ISBN 0-671-68120-6   CIP
ISBN 0-671-68364-0 (lib. bdg.)   AC
    ISBN 382-24674-8 (pbk)

Published by Silver Press, a division of
Silver Burdett Press, Inc.,
Simon & Schuster, Inc.,
Prentice Hall Bldg., Englewood Cliffs, NJ 07632.
Printed in the United States of America.

10 9 8 7 6 5 4 3 2

A Note to Parents

MY SILLY BOOKS are perfect for parents and children to share together. Each book is designed to introduce a beginning concept. Read each one first, just for fun. Encourage your child to look carefully. The illustrations contain additional details that reinforce concepts. Large, simple text encourages your preschool child to pick out words.

Now, look again–there's more to be found in the silly animal antics. Ask your child to think about what might come next. Be imaginative! Encourage your child to be creative and, most of all, have fun!

These silly pups and kittens
like to turn things upside down.

They fill the world with color
and they really paint the town!

The princess wakens early
and she combs her yellow hair.

Her handsome prince is near
but she can't find him anywhere.

Dan the Dreadful Dragon will eat anything that's green: lettuce, spinach, clover, peas,

green

pistachio ice cream!

Petronella the pink piggy
is a happy bride today...

pink

until her handsome piggy groom
starts nibbling the bouquet!

Queen Eleanor drinks grape juice
and she wears a purple dress.

purple

She always chews grape bubble gum
and makes a royal mess.

What a day! The sky is gray!
The rain begins to pour!

gray

But thanks to Ellie Elephant
the mice can play some more.

It's Randy Rabbit's birthday
but he's got a stomachache...

orange

from drinking all that orange juice
and eating too much cake!

Maxwell Monkey eats potatoes
as he swings among the trees.

Then he tosses big brown coconuts
at everything he sees!

Wanda wears her blue jeans
when she bakes blueberry pie.

blue

She flies up on her magic broom
to pile the berries high!

A hoot owl screeches. A bat flaps its wings.
A witch rides her broomstick. A nightingale sings.

The deep dark woods are black as night.
Hurry! Scurry! Hide in fright!

The polar bears won't sleep tonight.
They'd rather have a pillow fight.

With big, white pillows full of snow,
they make a giant blizzard blow.

Each night the merry monster
wears pajamas colored red.

red

She snacks on berries dipped in jam
and snuggles in her bed.

How many monsters wear red suspenders?

How many bumper cars have yellow fenders?

How many witches hold things that are blue?

How many white bears are looking at you?

Can you name all the colors of the rainbow?